cloverleaf books™

Our American Symbols

# Why Are There Stripes on the American Flag?

Martha E. H. Rustad

illustrated by Kyle Poling

M MILLBROOK PRESS · MINNEAPOLIS

For Dad and Mom, Joanne and Herman,
Donna and Ned, and Eva Jean and Jim
—K.P.

Millbrook Press
A division of Lerner Publishing Group, Inc.
241 First Avenue North
Minneapolis, MN 55401 USA

For reading levels and more information, look up this title at
www.lernerbooks.com.

Main body text set in Slappy Inline 18/28.
Typeface provided by T26.

Library of Congress Cataloging-in-Publication Data

Rustad, Martha E. H. (Martha Elizabeth Hillman), 1975–
    Why are there stripes on the American flag? / Martha E. H. Rustad ;
  illustrated by Kyle Poling.
        pages    cm. — (Cloverleaf books ™ — Our American symbols)
    Includes index.
    ISBN 978–1–4677–2140–0 (lib. bdg. : alk. paper)
    ISBN 978–1–4677–4773–8 (eBook)
    1.  Flags—United States—Juvenile literature.  I. Poling, Kyle, illustrator.
  II. Title.
  CR113.R86  2015
  929.9'20973—dc23                                    2013034226

Manufactured in the United States of America
1 – BP – 7/15/14

# TABLE OF CONTENTS

# Chapter One

# A Symbol of the United States

RRRIIIINNNGGG! Time for school!
Our teacher greets us. Everyone stands. We begin,
"I pledge allegiance to the flag . . ."

Charles raises his hand. "Wait! Mr. Gomez?" he says. "What does that mean?"

"And why do we put our hands on our hearts?" asks Khalil.

"Great questions," says Mr. Gomez. "Let's talk about the **American flag**."

The US flag is one of the oldest in the world. Only six countries have flags that are older: Austria, Denmark, Great Britain, the Netherlands, and Switzerland.

Mr. Gomez says the flag is a **symbol** for our **country**. "The United States of America became a country in **1776**. People worked together to make a new government. They wanted a symbol to show who they were."

**GRAND UNION FLAG**
(USED 1775–1777)

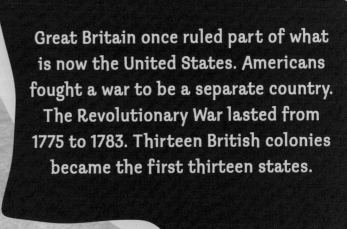

Great Britain once ruled part of what is now the United States. Americans fought a war to be a separate country. The Revolutionary War lasted from 1775 to 1783. Thirteen British colonies became the first thirteen states.

The Thirteen Colonies

"What's a symbol?" Ethan asks.

"A symbol is something that stands for something else," Mr. Gomez answers.

"Like a green light means go!" says Josie.

# Chapter Two
# Our Changing Flag

We learn that in 1777, American leaders decided how the flag should look. They wanted to use **red**, **white**, and **blue**. The red stands for **courage**. White stands for being **pure** and **good**. And blue stands for **fairness**.

**Flag Act of 1777**

Resolved, That the flag of the United States be made of thirteen stripes, alternate red and white: that the union be thirteen stars, white in a blue field, representing a new Constellation.

The Flag Act described the official US flag. Leaders signed the Flag Act on June 14, 1777. Each year, June 14 is honored as Flag Day.

The leaders also wanted to use star shapes on part of the flag. Our new country was like a new group of stars shining in the night sky.

Mr. Gomez shows us a picture of the first flag. "Why are there only **thirteen stars**?" asks Miles.

Mr. Gomez answers, "Because at first, the country had thirteen states."

1776

1777

At first, the flag wasn't always made the same way. One early design put the stars in a circle. Others put the 13 stars in rows.

1950-present

1814

"But our classroom flag has about a million stars!" says Hannah.

"Well, not quite that many," our teacher says. "Each time a new state joined our country, we added a star. Today we have **fifty states** and **fifty stars.**"

Mr. Gomez asks us what else we see when we look at the flag.

"Red and white stripes," answers Jamia. We count them.

Nicknames for the US flag include the Stars and Stripes, the Star-Spangled Banner, and Old Glory.

"Thirteen!" says Emi. "**Seven red** stripes and **six white** stripes."

"Yes," smiles our teacher. "Our flag has thirteen stripes to stand for . . ."

"The first thirteen states!" we say together.

# Chapter Three

# The Pledge of Allegiance

"But we still don't know what all those words mean!" says Xavier.

"Let's look at the pledge carefully," says Mr. Gomez.

*I pledge allegiance to the Flag of the United States of America . . .*

We learn that **allegiance** means "**friendship**" or "**loyalty.**" Saying those words is like promising to be a good friend to the flag!

"But how can you be friends with a flag?" asks Alex.

Our teacher laughs. "It's a way of saying you will **respect** the flag," he says.

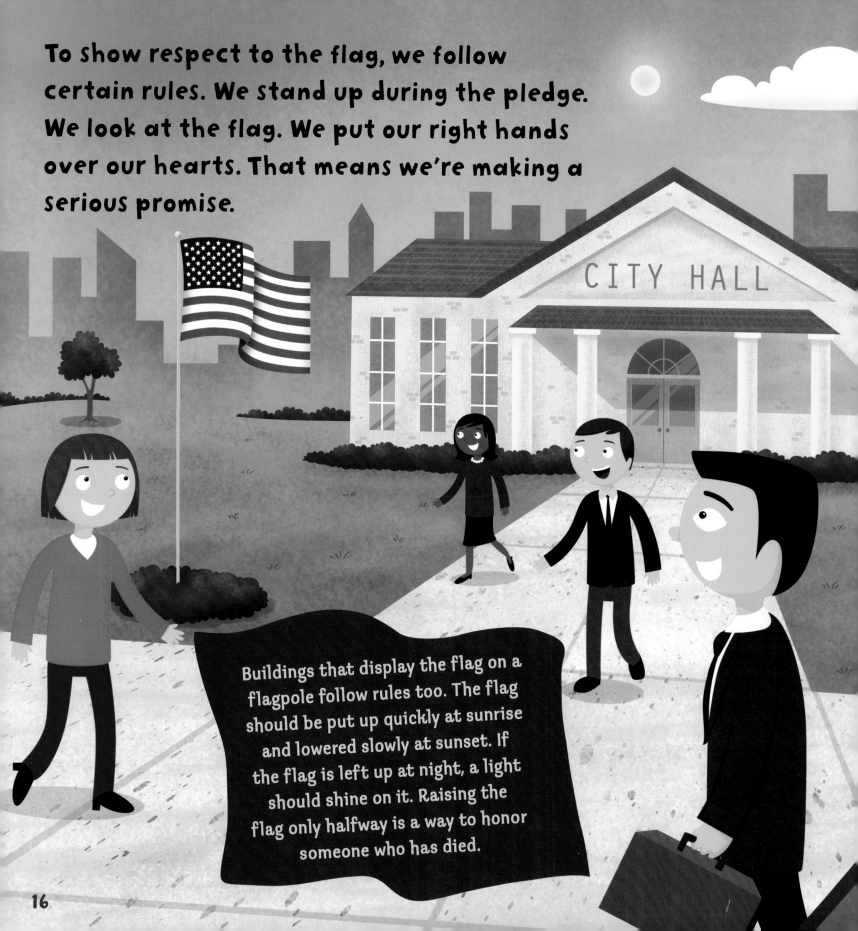

To show respect to the flag, we follow certain rules. We stand up during the pledge. We look at the flag. We put our right hands over our hearts. That means we're making a serious promise.

Buildings that display the flag on a flagpole follow rules too. The flag should be put up quickly at sunrise and lowered slowly at sunset. If the flag is left up at night, a light should shine on it. Raising the flag only halfway is a way to honor someone who has died.

We keep reading.

**And to the Republic for which it stands, . . .**

"A republic is the kind of government we have," Mr. Gomez explains. "In the US, people vote to choose leaders, instead of having a king or a queen. So this line is a promise to be **loyal** to our country too."

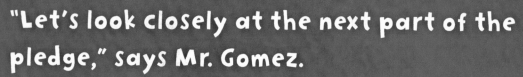

"Let's look closely at the next part of the pledge," says Mr. Gomez.

**One Nation under God, indivisible, . . .**

"*Indivisible* means something that can't be taken apart," he explains.

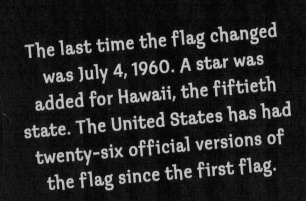

The last time the flag changed was July 4, 1960. A star was added for Hawaii, the fiftieth state. The United States has had twenty-six official versions of the flag since the first flag.

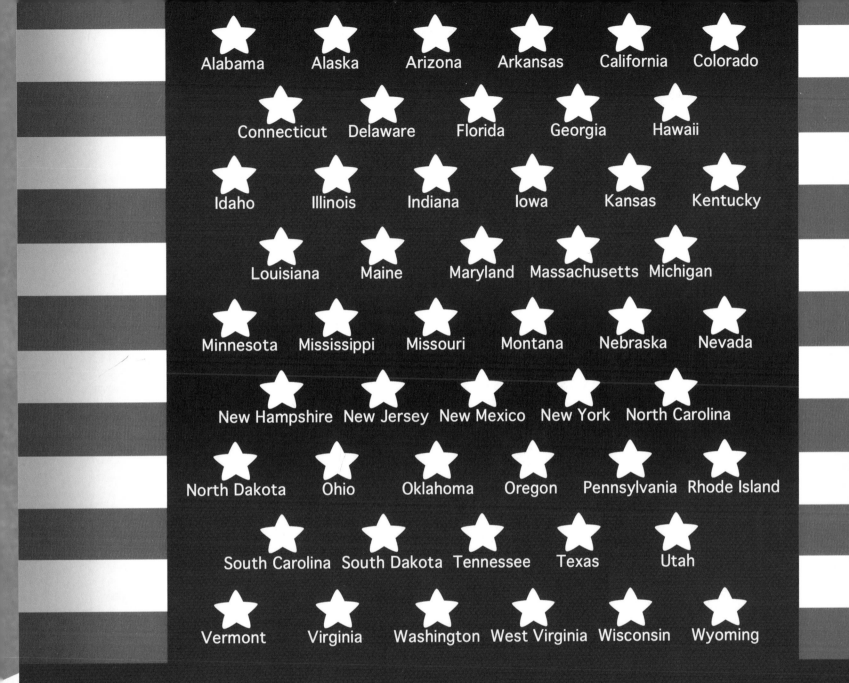

Alabama  Alaska  Arizona  Arkansas  California  Colorado

Connecticut  Delaware  Florida  Georgia  Hawaii

Idaho  Illinois  Indiana  Iowa  Kansas  Kentucky

Louisiana  Maine  Maryland  Massachusetts  Michigan

Minnesota  Mississippi  Missouri  Montana  Nebraska  Nevada

New Hampshire  New Jersey  New Mexico  New York  North Carolina

North Dakota  Ohio  Oklahoma  Oregon  Pennsylvania  Rhode Island

South Carolina  South Dakota  Tennessee  Texas  Utah

Vermont  Virginia  Washington  West Virginia  Wisconsin  Wyoming

He reminds us that we can do more when we work as a team.

"Like when we all help clean up!" says Sasha.

Our teacher nods. "Our country needs all fifty states. Even if we disagree, we stay together. The states are stronger together than apart."

19

Mr. Gomez asks Jordan to read the last line.
**With liberty and justice for all.**
"What does *liberty* mean?" asks Mr. Gomez.
Becky raises her hand. **"Being free!"**
Our teacher says, "Right! And *justice* means **'fairness.'** What does fairness mean to you?"

The American flag even flies on the moon!

"Getting the same size cookie as my sister!" says Grace.

"Getting equal turns on the monkey bars at recess!" Leif says.

Together we say the Pledge of Allegiance again.
And then we go out for recess!

# Make Your Own Flag

Every country and every state has a flag.
Each flag shows symbols that tell about that place.
Make a flag that tells about you: yesterday, today, and tomorrow.

**What You Need:**
Paper
Crayons, colored pencils, or markers

1) Choose a flag design. Plan to use different symbols in different sections of the flag. Draw the outline on your paper.

2) Think about a favorite memory. What symbol could go with it? For example, if you took a trip to the mountains, you might draw a mountain.

3) Think about a favorite activity. If you like to swim, you could draw a pair of goggles. If you enjoy reading, you might draw a book.

4) Think about something you hope will happen someday. Do you hope to travel to the moon? Would you love to have a pet bird? Draw a picture that shows your wish.

# GLOSSARY

**allegiance:** loyalty to a group or cause, or friendship for a group or person

**colony:** land that is ruled by another country

**constellation:** a group of stars

**government:** a group of people that make rules for a country

**indivisible:** something that cannot be separated

**justice:** fairness

**liberty:** freedom

**republic:** a kind of government where people vote to choose leaders

**respect:** to have a good opinion of something or someone

**symbol:** an object that stands for something else

## BOOKS

**Gaspar, Joe.** *The Flag.* New York: PowerKids Press, 2014.
Find out more about the flag.

**Swanson, June.** *I Pledge Allegiance.* Minneapolis: Carolrhoda Books, 2002.
Learn how the pledge became an important symbol of the United States.

## WEBSITES

**About the Flag**
http://www.va.gov/kids/k-5/multicontent.asp?intPageId=8
This website from the Department of Veterans Affairs tells how to display the flag.

**Flags of the World**
https://www.cia.gov/library/publications/the-world-factbook/docs/flagsoftheworld.html
This website from the CIA shows each country's flag.

**Symbols of the US Government**
http://bensguide.gpo.gov/k-2/symbols/index.html
This website from the US Government Printing Office tells about famous symbols of the US government.

LERNER *e* SOURCE™

Expand learning beyond the printed book. Download free, complementary educational resources for this book from our website, www.lerneresource.com.